Getting Creative with

FAB
LAB™

Creating with

MILLING
MACHINES

JASON PORTERFIELD

rosen publishing's
rosen
central®

Published in 2017 by The Rosen Publishing Group, Inc.
29 East 21st Street, New York, NY 10010

First Edition

Library of Congress Cataloging-in-Publication Data

Names: Porterfield, Jason, author.
Title: Creating with milling machines / Jason Porterfield.
Description: First edition. | New York : Rosen Publishing, 2017. | Series: Getting creative with Fab Lab | Audience: Grades 5 to 8. | Includes bibliographical references and index.
Identifiers: LCCN 2016022564 | ISBN 9781499465068 (library bound)
Subjects: LCSH: Milling machinery—Juvenile literature. | Makerspaces—Juvenile literature. | Technological innovations—Juvenile literature.
Classification: LCC TJ1345 .P67 2017 | DDC 621.9/1—dc23
LC record available at https://lccn.loc.gov/2016022564

Manufactured in China

Contents

Introduction

Fabrication laboratories, or Fab Labs, originated at MIT's Center for Bits and Atoms before being introduced to high schools, colleges, and community centers around the country and the world. They provide a hands-on learning environment where students can design, build, and innovate using cutting-edge machines and equipment. Fab Labs are part of a larger "maker" movement, in which people create projects of all kinds from scratch. Collaboration, community, and sharing of resources are central to both maker and Fab Lab ideology.

Fab Labs are the new generation of shop and art classes, allowing students to "make (almost) anything," according to the MIT class that spurred the development of Fab Lab. The Fab Foundation describes the workspaces as places "to play, to create, to learn, to mentor, to invent." Projects require self-directed learning, creative thinking, and problem solving—qualities that will serve students well in contexts beyond Fab Lab.

Most Fab Labs include a suite of equipment that is consistent across all Fab Labs in order to facilitate sharing of knowledge throughout a global network. These include programming tools,

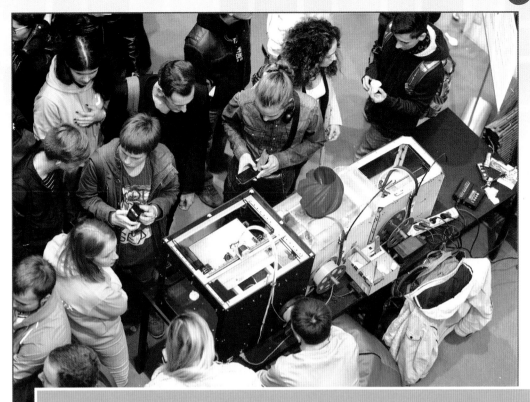

Fab Labs can be found across the globe. Here, visitors to a university science festival congregate around the exhibit hosted by the St. Petersburg State Polytechnic University Fab Lab.

a 3D printer, a laser cutter, a vinyl cutter, a router, and a milling machine, which is sometimes called a "desktop mill." The milling machine is a piece of equipment that cuts and carves away material from a larger workpiece, such as a rectangle of circuit board or a piece of metal that is going to be made into jewelry. Milling machines can be used to create custom pieces or create prototypes intended to be mass-produced later on in the manufacturing process.

Chapter ONE

INTRODUCING FAB LAB

Are you a maker? Do you look forward to hanging out in a hackerspace in your free time? Are you an aspiring DIY tinkerer or is product development more in line with your interests—or do you enjoy dabbling a little in both artistic and STEM endeavors?

If you don't follow all of these terms, you probably haven't yet acquainted yourself with the maker movement, a still-evolving set of ideas and approaches toward creating new things and repurposing old ones. The maker movement is innovative—it relies on the internet to spread ideas and involves high-tech tools. At the same time, it incorporates the old tradition of people doing hands-on work on the projects, crafts, hobbies, and inventions that interest them. The maker movement is connected to the Do It Yourself (DIY) approach to creating and repairing things, but there's also a collaborative aspect. Makers consult, collaborate, and share online and in the workspace. Making is often a Do It With Others (DIWO) endeavor.

Creative Spaces

Before the industrial age, many people made a living as artisans, craftsmen, tinkerers, and small-time inventors who created goods. This changed with the Industrial Revolution, which introduced mass production of goods. Artisans who made unique pieces were largely replaced by factory workers. Today, even as people appreciate the convenience and variety of affordable manufactured products, interest has increased in unique items with significance beyond their appearance or function.

Some people want to be makers of goods rather than mere consumers. Others are attracted to items that are hand-made or locally produced, providing a market for makers interested in earning money out of their making. The internet offers the means to display and sell these products around the world.

Technological advances have helped fuel the maker movement. The internet revolution made information accessible worldwide. People

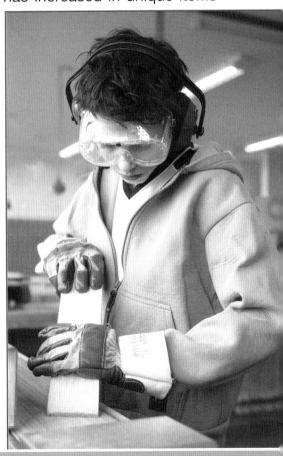

Many makers derive satisfaction from creating items and designs from scratch rather than settling for disposable, mass-produced goods readily available commercially.

became involved in new activities such as programming, online research, and social media facilitated by the world wide web. Since the early twenty-first century, innovative new fabrication tools and software have been developed that allow ordinary people to design and create products on a small scale that in the past would only have been possible in labs run by big companies. The next frontier being explored is the internet of things—devices and products that collect data and communicate with other objects. These range from the large-scale, such as smart houses, to everyday products, such as smart clothing. Some of the breakthroughs in smart gadgets will undoubtedly come from engineers working in fabrication workspaces.

MAKE: MAGAZINE

In 2005, the first issue of *Make:* magazine was published. The publication arrived at a perfect time for wannabe makers who were interested in learning to use new cutting-edge fabrication tools and connecting with other makers across the country and around the world. The magazine offered instructions for DIY projects, many of them highly complex yet affordable for home tinkerers. Today, *Make:* is available in print and digital subscriptions. Non-subscribers can learn about the maker movement at the magazine's website, http://makezine.com.

Maker Faires have become internationally popular. Maker Faire Rome, held in 2015, is the third largest Maker Faire, after the New York and San Francisco events.

As interest in the maker movement surged, the publisher of *Make:* launched Maker Faire. The first Maker Faire was held in California in 2006 and gave makers an opportunity to showcase what they'd made. Maker Faire has since grown into annual extravaganzas held across the world with exhibits, shows, presentations, and large-scale demonstrations of cutting-edge and inventive projects. As described on the makerfaire.com site, "Maker Faire is primarily designed to be forward-looking, showcasing makers who are exploring new forms and new technologies. But it's not just for the novel in technical fields; Maker Faire features innovation and experimentation across the spectrum of science, engineering, art, performance and craft."

But makers aren't just engineers and tech geeks. Many makers are artists, crafters, and practical DIY enthusiasts. They might make sculptures, hand-woven cloth, or strawberry jam. They may use novel technology in the production, or maybe not. Makers also utilize many of the tools found in traditional workshops, such as equipment for working with metal or wood.

These makers and their tools come together in makerspaces, which provide resources and the opportunity for collaboration. These places combine aspects of an artist's studio, machine shop, and computer lab. The makerspace might be affiliated with a school or community center, or it might be an independent organization. Although policies and procedures vary from one makerspace to another, members often pay a set fee for use of the equipment. There may be formal classes, especially in makerspaces used by kids and teens, but makerspaces are more about self-directed learning than following a lesson led by a teacher. Groups of people with common interests may get together to share their knowledge, whether they're building their own computers, inventing musical instruments, or using engraving to customize cell phone cases and other products.

Another innovative type of workspace is the hackerspace. The "hackers" who tinker and create in a hackerspace are not the same group as computer hackers who commit cybercrimes. Here, to "hack" something means to find a novel solution to a problem or a new method of completing an everyday task, often involving an ingenious, tech-savvy approach. The terms *makerspace* and *hackerspace* are sometimes used interchangeably, but knowledge of computer hardware, software, and electronics are more central to a hackerspace than a makerspace.

Fabulous Fabrication

A Fab Lab is a very specific type of makerspace. For one thing, the name *Fab Lab* is trademarked. Fab Labs are supported by a nonprofit foundation, Fab Foundation, which works to promote digital fabrication on educational, organizational, and business levels. On its website, the foundation states its mission to be, "Provide access to the tools, the knowledge and the financial means to educate, innovate and invent using technology and digital fabrication to allow anyone to make (almost) anything, and thereby creating opportunities to improve lives and livelihoods around the world." The educational and organizational aspects help to create a network that can create cutting-edge business opportunities and carve out new markets for products and services.

Fab Labs are part of the foundation's educational and organizational outreach efforts. Although Fab Labs aren't all identical to each other, they share several core capabilities, including certain machines and programming tools. The Fab Foundation provides resources to help with the establishment of new labs and support existing labs. Organizations interested in starting up a Fab Lab can learn about purchasing equipment, training lab managers, and establishing programs. The Fab Foundation also evaluates what works best in various labs so that other Fab Labs can adopt similar practices. It also provides a network so that people working in Fab Labs across the world can connect with other labs.

A workspace must meet four criteria in order to qualify as a Fab Lab. It must allow public access. It must comply with the Fab Lab charter that outlines certain requirements and responsibilities. It must offer certain equipment and capabilities. And it must take part in the global Fab Lab network.

THE ORIGINS OF FAB LAB

In 2003, Neil Gershenfeld, a computer science professor at MIT, introduced a new class called How to Make (Almost) Anything. Gershenfeld is the director of MIT's Center for Bits and Atoms (CBA), which describes itself as "an interdisciplinary initiative exploring the boundary between computer science and physical science." The class was meant to teach students how to use CBA equipment. It was a much greater success than anticipated. Students didn't just want to learn how to use the tools, they wanted to make things that would have a personal touch to them.

The CBA expanded on the results of that class by taking digital fabrication to the community through an outreach program. Instead of just teaching the concepts, however, a team set up an entire workshop in a Boston technology center. The goal was to provide a broad range of high-tech equipment at a cost that would be affordable for a community organization—the cost of this first Fab Lab was about $70,000. The project proved hugely popular, helping users

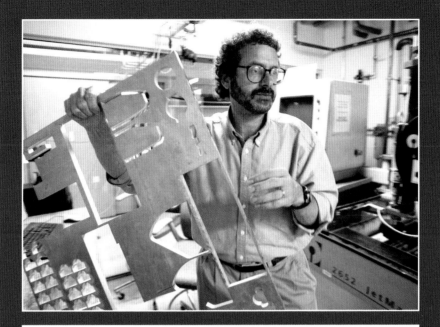

Neil Gershenfeld displays a piece of aluminum which has gone through a precision milling machine at the MIT Fab Lab in Cambridge, Massachusetts.

gain technical skills while they had fun in a space that promoted self-directed learning.

The CBA didn't initially plan to transform Fab Lab into a global phenomenon. But people from a Ghanaian community in Boston expressed interest in taking Fab Lab to their country. The third Fab Lab was established in Africa, in the Ghanaian town of Sekondi-Takoradi. Today, there are over six hundred Fab Labs in over a hundred nations worldwide. The program has expanded to include Fab Foundation, founded to support Fab Labs, which is affiliated with Fab Academy and other related endeavors.

On its website, the Fab Foundation describes one purpose of a Fab Lab as "a technical prototyping platform for innovation and invention, providing stimulus for local entrepreneurship." People can visit a Fab Lab to create a product, design, or process that solves a problem or fills a need. They might fine-tune the details of the product and finalize a prototype—an early model. Once they have a successful final result, they could commercialize it, perhaps by having a product mass-produced or starting a business that provides a service.

Increasingly, however, Fab Labs have been established for educational purposes. They offer a hands-on approach to teaching STEM (science, technology, engineering, and math) concepts to students. Fab Labs are found in schools on all levels from elite universities to technical colleges to middle schools, as well as libraries and community centers.

Tools for Creating

A model Fab Lab can be visited at Chicago's Museum of Science and Industry. This Fab Lab features a workspace slightly smaller than 2,000 square feet (180 square meters) in area, which is designed to accommodate twenty to thirty users. Many school and community Fab Lab facilities are smaller in scale.

The lab offers fifteen CAD work stations—"CAD" means "computer-aided design." Anyone beginning a Fab Lab project generally starts out by sitting down in front of a computer. Once someone has a concept in mind, it can be entered into a computer program used to design the final product. The software allows the user to model its appearance and run simulations of its process or function. These programs are easy to master quickly, but complex and versatile enough to allow a huge variety

On July 9, 2015, a student works on CAD software for fabrication during a summer school course at the Museum of Science and Industry's Wanger Family Fab Lab, in Chicago, Illinois.

of designs of various kinds. The software then instructs the machines in constructing the product. Fab Labs are intended to be collaborative and interconnected, so anybody working in one Fab Lab should be able to share their files with anybody else in Fab Labs across the world without having software compatibility problems. Nonetheless, not all Fab Labs use the same programs.

Most Fab Labs have a handful of machines in common. These include 3D printers, laser cutters, vinyl cutters, routers, and milling machines. Labs generally have one or more of each. Most of the pieces of equipment are desktop models that do not require much space, and most run off of regular electricity outlets.

The 3D printer is the most novel and popular machine for many Fab Lab visitors. These printers were first developed in the 1980s, but they've only became widely available for home and classroom use since the 2000s. The 3D printing process is sometimes called "additive manufacturing." As with all Fab Lab machines, a project begins with a design created on a computer. The machine applies material in successive layers in order to create a three-dimensional object. Many Fab Lab newcomers are fascinated by watching the machine fabricate the product. Most desktop printers use plastic; industrial printers can create products out of many other materials, including metal, wood, ceramic, and wax. Typical objects for demonstration tend to be knick-knacks and novelties, but 3D printers have many advanced and potentially revolutionary applications. The medical industry has worked to develop organs and tissues printed with 3D printers. Car parts can be created with 3D printers, and, controversially, so can firearms. In 2016, a college student straightened his own teeth using 3D printed aligners—not to be tried by novices.

The laser cutter uses a laser for highly precise cutting or engraving of flat shapes. It can work on a variety of materials, including wood, acrylic, glass, fabric, rubber, leather, marble, and paper. After the user has finalized the design, he or she places the material to be cut or engraved on the machine's work surface. The laser settings are included in the instructions sent to the machine. The laser points downward toward the material being cut and moves along the lines specified in the design. The laser cutter can be used to make flat pieces such as puzzles or panels of customized cloth. It can also produce 2D components that can be pieced together into a larger 3D structure.

A vinyl cutter cuts shapes out of pieces of vinyl. Some machines can also work with sheets of other thin material, such as fabric, cardboard, or metal. After the user has finalized the design, the machine executes it by moving a blade from side to side—the blade can also turn—while the material moves back and forth under it. The vinyl cutter can be used to make signs, labels, stickers, decals for T-shirts, and decorations of all kinds, as well as circuits and antennas.

The largest machine in most Fab Labs is the wood router. The router cuts and engraves pieces of wood—and sometimes other materials such as plastic or some metals—placed on a large platform called a cutting bed. The spindle, on which a cutting tool is mounted, moves up, down, and across in order to

A woman shapes a piece of wood. Fab Labs include traditional shop tools for working pieces by hand as well as cutting-edge equipment.

carve the design or cut out pieces. Routers can be used to make pieces of furniture, signs, components of musical instruments, and decorative pieces.

The milling machine is another key piece of Fab Lab equipment. Like the router, the milling machine carves wood or other materials using a spindle, but it is not restricted to a flat surface. The milling machine works through the opposite process from that of additive manufacturing used by the 3D printer—instead, it removes material from a larger workpiece.

Many of the products fabricated by machines in the Fab Lab require additional work in order to achieve the end result. The user might have to file down parts of a piece produced by a 3D printer or assemble shapes cut out by a laser cutter or router. A piece of cut vinyl might contain unwanted sections that must be punched out.

The museum model Fab Lab in Chicago has separate stations for the router, the laser cutters, and the 3D printers. The vinyl cutters and the milling machines share an electronics workbench. The facility also features a soldering and electronics assembly station; a molding, casting, and silkscreen station; and ample work and storage space.

Chapter TWO

KNOW YOUR MILLING MACHINE

Milling machine is a broad term that describes a piece of equipment used to cut away material from a larger workpiece. This is done using a spinning cutting tool that removes material in small chips or shavings. There are many different kinds of mills. There are huge industrial machines and smaller models for home shops. Milling machines vary, depending on how they operate and the types of tools they use.

The earliest milling machines were developed in the nineteenth century, and they quickly became essential in manufacturing. In 1936, the improved "Bridgeport milling machine" became the dominant type used by machinists. By the 1940s, automation was common in milling operations. This was a precursor to computer numerical control (CNC), in which computers direct the machine's operations. All types of Fab Lab equipment are CNC machines. In fact, the first numerically controlled (NC) mill was created at MIT in 1952. CAD programs were developed in the

1960s to create the drawings and models used by the machines, and computer numerical control was introduced in the 1970s.

Milling Machine Basics

There are many different brands and types of milling machines. The machines used in Fab Labs are CNC desktop mills. They are smaller than the industrial mills used in machine shops. Many of them have transparent covers or doors that can be closed when the machine is being used. New desktop mills with enhanced capabilities or improved software are regularly being introduced to the market.

The basic model recommended by the Fab Lab Foundation is the Roland MonoFab SRM-20. It's a small piece of equipment with external dimensions of about 17 inches (430 mm) in length, width, and height. It can work on a piece of material about 8 x 6 x 2.4 inches (200 x 150 x 60 mm) in size. This mill can cut a variety of relatively soft materials, such as modeling wax, foam, and a variety of different kinds of plastic.

The MonoFab SRM-20 is a three-axis machine. The number of axes describes the movement of the cutting operations. Some machines move just the cutting tool. Others also move the workpiece itself, which is tightly secured in place. A three-axis machine cuts from three directions: X, Y, and Z. In the X dimension, the piece is cut from left and right; in Y, forward and back; and in Z, up and down.

Another recommended model is the more advanced Roland MDX-40A CNC Mill, described as a subtractive rapid prototyping system. It can mill larger pieces than the MonoFab SRM-20— about 12 x 12 x 4 inches (300 x 300 x 100 mm). An optional feature is a scanning unit. If the user places an object inside the unit, the scanner can create a digital 3D file of the object.

Makeda Stephenson uses a computer-controlled milling machine at the MIT Fab Lab to create a component of a fantastical flight simulator designed to fly over an alien planet.

In some cases, the machine can then mill a reproduction of the piece. This model also has an optional fourth rotary axis, meaning that the workpiece can be positioned so that it can be turned as it is cut.

3D SCANNERS

Creating a 3D model to be fabricated using a milling machine or 3D printer can be a complex and lengthy process. If there's already a similar object that the user wants to replicate or use as the basis for a piece, it might be possible to obtain a digital model using a 3D scanner.

A relatively new technology, 3D scanners collect data about the object being scanned, such as shape and sometimes color, and stores it as a file. There are many different models available that use various approaches to capture a 3D rendering of a target object. Most are very expensive, and the technology is still in development. Prices will probably fall in the next few years even as capabilities improve. Handheld 3D scanners already exist, and smartphones of the future might be able to scan objects in 3D just as today's phones can snap pictures.

Models created with 3D scanners are useful in many fields. They can be used for reverse engineering, such as when a user fabricates a copy of a scanned object. They have applications for architects designing a project for a specific location and for engineers working on a piece with complex shapes. They're used in the entertainment industry for creating special effects in movies and video games. These 3D scanners also create models of historic artifacts and art objects for educational and archiving purposes.

A third recommended model is the much larger and more powerful Roland MDX-540 Milling Machine, which advertises that it creates prototypes that are fully functional. It's capable of milling wood and some metals other than iron in addition to softer materials.

Designing for the Milling Machine

The first step in putting the milling machine to work is to come up with a design. This is done using a CAD program that draws the design—a CAD program is essentially a toolkit that creates a file describing the piece. CAD software is used in many fields,

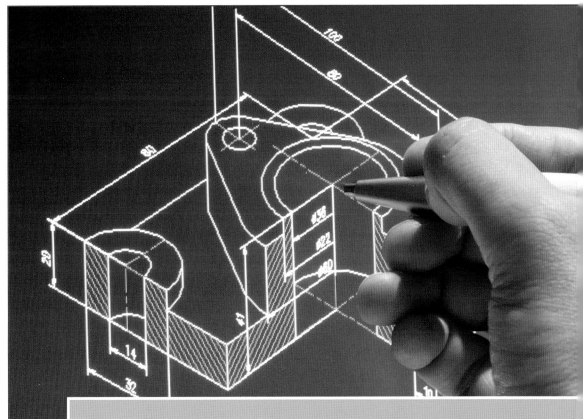

Computer-Aided Design (CAD) software is used to create and modify designs and models, as well as run real-world simulations to test performance.

from architecture to engineering to product design. Good CAD programs can be very expensive, but there are free programs available that are sophisticated and user-friendly. Fab Labs tend to promote open source software. A Fab Lab adviser can tell newcomers about the software used in the workspace and recommend the program best suited for modeling a piece intended for milling machine fabrication. Files created with one CAD program can often be opened with another program, but they're not always compatible.

Generating a CAD design or model is only the first step toward starting up the milling machine to fabricate the piece. Milling machines do not read CAD drawings directly. The content of the

A designer manipulates an image of a component using CAD software. CAD is used in many fields, from engineering to architecture to fashion design.

CAD file must be converted to an NC programming language called G-Code, which directs the mill as it manufactures a piece.

Computer aided manufacturing (CAM) software is used to convert the CAD file into G-Code. CAM programs consider factors such as cutting depth, speed, and tool selection for different parts of the job. The user will also consider during this process whether the milling machine is capable of completing the required cutting paths to fabricate the piece as designed in the CAD drawing. As with CAD software, there are many CAM programs available, both for sale and free. Some programs combine CAD and CAM functions. It can be a challenge to master CAD and CAM software, and some experts recommend concentrating on one before tackling the other instead of trying to learn both at once.

Once the G-Code has been generated, it's time to transfer the G-Code file to the milling machine, which may contain its own computer or may be connected to a separate computer. The user must also prepare the workpiece and secure it appropriately to the milling machine—for example, by clamping it to the work platform. Most of the fabrication process is controlled by the computer, but there may be some hands-on tasks for the user, such as changing cutting tools.

It may seem that Fab Lab machines can make anything the user dreams up, but an important part of using the equipment effectively is recognizing its limitations. A milling machine cannot cut away material inside the workpiece, for example. It can only remove material from the outside. If a project requires cavities with parts inside of them, the user may have to use ingenuity to design two or more pieces that can be milled separately and then assemble them afterward.

ABOUT OPEN SOURCE

Fab Lab and many other makerspaces and hackerspaces emphasize their support for open source software and programs. But what exactly does "open source" mean? And why is open source software so significant that some organizations and individuals make a special effort to champion it?

To start with, open source software is free to the user. The source code used to create the programs are included as well. Any user can alter the source code. This means that if you see a way that the program can be improved, you can modify the code to do so. This sets open source software apart from proprietary software that is sold commercially, which usually carry licenses with conditions that restrict the user's right to view and change source code. Open source software is also licensed, but these licenses often permit users to modify and redistribute programs, and to profit from selling those modified programs.

Supporters of open source software tout the many benefits of the practice. Pragmatically, it can make good business sense. Instead of having a team of developers exclusively work to improve a product, anybody in the world can help out by fixing bugs and adding enhancements. In this way, it works to build a community of people engaged together in fuelling innovation—a good match for Fab Lab's ideology and goals.

Which Fab Lab Machine Is Right for You?

As the user works on the design for a piece and finalizes the CAD drawings, the question may arise of whether the milling machine is really the best piece of equipment to fabricate the item. For some designs, the appropriate piece of equipment is obvious. If someone is working with medium-sized sheets of thin material, the vinyl cutter is the best choice. Likewise, the laser cutter is best for engraving or cutting sheets of slightly thicker material. The milling machine can do engraving, but that's not one of its most core functions. The CNC router and the milling machine perform similar operations—they both cut away from the original workpiece—but routers are generally preferred for large, flat stock.

The milling machine and the 3D printer, however, both fabricate relatively small, detailed pieces. The two machines are even sometimes described as competing means of fabrication. This view might come as a surprise, since 3D printers are generally seen as highly futuristic pieces of equipment, whereas the milling machine continues to be an essential machining tool in manufacturing even as desktop mills find their way into Fab Labs and other makerspaces.

There are advantages and disadvantages to both means of fabrication. One of the greatest advantages of using a milling machine is the range of materials it works, from plastic to wood to metal. Three-D printers are largely limited to plastics and resins, which are weaker and less permanent. Milling machines often yield a higher degree of accuracy and precision than 3D printers. They're generally faster, as well, although the speed

Milling machines can fabricate highly precise parts from wood and many other materials that are used as components for a wide variety of purposes.

of both machines depends on the piece being fabricated. Production using a 3D printer is sometimes less expensive, however, and 3D printers are better suited for many novel uses. Experts weighing the pros and cons of the two types of machines often conclude that both are great to have in a Fab Lab. In addition, both 3D printers and milling machines are becoming more versatile, user-friendly, and affordable as technology advances and demand for the machines continues to encourage innovation.

Chapter
THREE

MAKING WITH THE MILLING MACHINE

Watching a milling machine at work makes a job look easy. The spindle moves smoothly and efficiently, with each pass leaving behind worked material far more precisely cut than a human being could manage. Hopefully, seeing a milling machine in action makes you want to design and fabricate your own pieces. But if you have the opposite reaction of thinking that the milling machine is more complicated and difficult than you can manage, take heart. There are milling machine projects for makers of all levels. Fab Lab aims to create a fun learning environment, and most newcomers come to relish the challenge.

Learning the Ropes

Learning to use a milling machine can be challenging. You'll do a lot of learning through trial and error as you work through your first projects. You will probably want to start with a fairly small, basic design for your first effort so that you can observe how

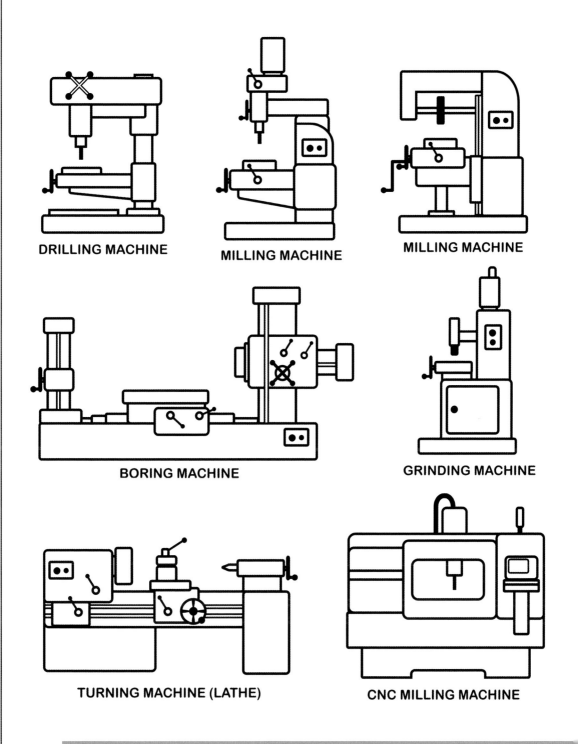

DRILLING MACHINE

MILLING MACHINE

MILLING MACHINE

BORING MACHINE

GRINDING MACHINE

TURNING MACHINE (LATHE)

CNC MILLING MACHINE

Machine tools work metal and other materials by cutting and other processes. Today, Computer Numeric Control (CNC) allows greater control and precision.

the software and machine work. Some experts recommend trying out a design in which the head moves only in the X and Y dimensions while you're first learning how the machine moves. You may also want to choose a soft material that's easy to work. Harder materials require greater care and expertise in choosing the settings for cutting the piece. For your later projects, you can customize your work more carefully and experiment with more complex pieces.

FAB LAB SAFETY

Before you leap into your first Fab Lab project, acquaint yourself thoroughly with safety protocol. Fab Lab equipment is designed to be safe and user-friendly, but don't forget that you're using high-powered machinery that can be potentially dangerous if used improperly or without proper regard for safety. Be careful when handling equipment, especially the cutting tools. Don't put your hands anywhere near the cutting tool when the mill is in use, and know how to operate the emergency stop. Remember that the mill creates debris that could be ejected quickly or have sharp edges. The cutting tool also creates heat as it works material, and you should take care to avoid burning yourself. Lab fires are unlikely, but there's always a possibility when working with electronics and electrical equipment. If you're working with large, heavy, pieces of material, take care in lifting and transporting pieces. Use proper gear such as safety glasses, gloves, and hearing protection when required. Your Fab Lab may have restrictions for clothing and jewelry that is allowed when you're working

Fab Labs prioritize the safety of users. You should be familiar with protective gear and know the procedures for the safe operation of Fab Lab equipment.

near machines. Acquaint yourself with emergency procedures—know the location of fire extinguishers and the nearest emergency exits.

If you have any doubts about proper use of equipment, ask someone. Using the mill incorrectly could put your safety at risk and possibly damage the machine. Your Fab Lab probably has procedures for training people before they're permitted to use the machines on their own. Some Fab Labs and makerspaces require that newcomers undergo steps to receive authorization or certification for a particular piece of equipment. This may involve taking a class or learning how to use it from someone who's experienced with using the machine.

If you've never seen a milling machine in action before, you might be taken aback when you start it up. Unlike 3D printers, which are quiet and produce no waste, milling machines can be loud, and they create dust and scrap material. Even though manufacturers try to minimize the noise level, any machine capable of milling metal will not do so quietly. Also, although the fabrication is rapid compared to older methods, the machine isn't fast. Be prepared for the process to take at least an hour, probably longer. You may have to change tools at various points if your milling machine doesn't have an automatic tool changer.

Don't be disappointed if your first efforts aren't perfect. Using a milling machine requires learning about both computer code and the mechanical aspects of the machine. Some experts even recommend that aspiring machinists learn to use a milling mill manually in order to better understand how it works. In a Fab Lab, however, you'll probably start out by mostly following a preexisting design as you acquaint yourself with the programs and controls. Maybe your first try will turn out great, or maybe you'll immediately see room for improvement next time.

What Can You Make?

Milling machine enthusiasts often say that it's possible to make just about anything with a desktop mill. But with such a huge variety of options, where do you start? Look around your Fab Lab. You'll probably see demo pieces that other people have made. If the Fab Lab is affiliated with your school, there are probably periods of formal instruction in addition to time for hands-on learning. If your Fab Lab is part of a community center, staff or volunteers probably lead introductory sessions on using the different kinds of machines.

Explore books, magazines, and websites related to your interests in making things. Your Fab Lab can provide some places to find resources, and you can search on your own at the library and on the internet. You'll find both general interest discussion of making and hacking as well as technical descriptions of projects and skills. Sites such as Instructables.com (another MIT endeavor) offer a place for makers to share their designs and creations. CNC manuals and educational materials can help you learn and master the computer and mechanical aspects of using a milling machine. Videos at sites such as YouTube offer clips

Milling machines can work a wide variety of materials, which may be obtained at the Fab Lab, at a local shop, or from online sources.

of milling machines at work. Books and websites on design can introduce new ways of thinking about how to solve problems with results that are both functional and elegant. Check out general resources on the types of making that interest you, whether it's technology, arts, crafts, or traditional shop projects.

You may also wonder where you'll obtain the materials for your projects. Fab Labs provide some materials, either free or for a nominal fee. You can also search for what you need at hobby shops, craft shops, and hardware stores. Internet sites can offer more difficult-to-find items—make sure that you're dealing with a reputable seller.

Milling machines are great for making jewelry, knickknacks, and personalized practical items or unique novelties, from coasters to a modern version of the "turner's cube," an old-fashioned training exercise for apprentice machinists. Today, internet entrepreneurs use milling machines to create unique pieces and sell them on online marketplaces such as Etsy. These types of projects can also be easy and fun projects for beginners. You can start with nearly any material that can be worked by the machine in your Fab Lab. Milling machines can fabricate objects of all kinds from scratch or be used for detail work, such as engraving a bracelet.

Milling machines also provide the means of making machined parts for larger, more difficult projects, whether you're working on your own robot, a musical instrument, an art installation, or restoration work on a car. Maybe you're even constructing a CNC milling machine from scratch—it's a popular project among some DIY enthusiasts. CNC milling machines can make strong, precisely cut parts from a variety of materials. If you need custom gears or fastenings for your project, you can mill them yourself.

In particular, milling machines are ideal for fabrication of one specific component of many DIY projects that requires a great

ALL ABOUT PROTOTYPES

Many CNC milling machine companies tout the advantages of their machines in prototyping. Rapid prototyping. Highly accurate prototypes. Full functioning prototypes. But what exactly is a prototype, and why is prototyping such a big deal in discussing milling machines?

A prototype is a pre-production model of a product. A prototype can be a single part or a complete manufactured article—a prototype car, for example, is a novel model that demonstrates cutting-edge technology or a new design. Prototyping is usually a long process, although technological advances have made it easier. To begin with, the inventor comes up with a concept. Next, the concept is turned into a design and, if applicable, a physical product. Sometimes a rough prototype is adequate to demonstrate the product's general appearance. In other cases, the prototype must be fine-tuned many times until the version is finalized and tested. This is the part of the process in which a milling machine's capabilities are valuable. In the past, only big industrial machine shops would have been able to create sleek working prototypes. Makerspaces such as Fab Labs allow anybody to become a prospective inventor.

Often, the next step is presenting the prototype to prospective investors, business partners, and manufacturers. (The final product to be sold probably won't be manufactured using a milling machine—it will likely be mass-produced using a faster, cheaper process.) If they like what they see, it might soon be on the market for consumers to buy.

deal of precision: printed circuit boards (PCBs). A printed circuit board is the base that supports the components of an electrical circuit used in electronic devices. The board itself consists of a conductive copper layer coating a rigid, inert board. Boards are often coated on both sides or contain multiple layers. The electrical components, such as capacitors, resistors, and diodes, are mounted and connected on the board.

The first step in milling your own PCB is designing the electronic circuit on the computer. Next, you cut down a piece of

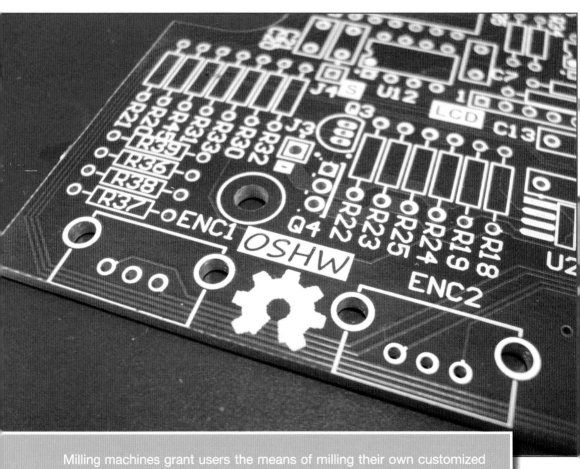

Milling machines grant users the means of milling their own customized printed circuit boards (PCBs). This one displays the Open Source Hardware (OSHW) logo.

board to the appropriate size, clean it, and secure it for milling. The machine then drills the holes for the components and carves away some of the copper coating, leaving behind the conductive paths as specified on the design. After the board has been milled, you solder on the electrical components. The result is a customized PCB for your device.

Another key use for milling machines is the production of molds. Molds are used in manufacturing processes, and they can be simple or difficult to make, depending on how intricate the design. Commercial products made using molds are all around you, from your toothbrush to the parts under the hood of your car. A mold is a hollow form containing an interior shape. Often, it consists of two halves that are pressed together. Liquid material, such as plastic, ceramic, or molten metal, is introduced into the mold. There are different types of molding—in injection molding, for example, the material is injected into the hollow cavity through an opening. Once the piece is set, it is removed from the mold, often by separating the two halves.

For a fun project, use your milling machine to make a mold using food-grade materials, such as wax for the model and silicon for the mold itself. You can pour melted chocolate into the two halves of the mold and create customized chocolate treats.

Chapter
FOUR

TECHNOLOGICAL EMPOWERMENT

Fab Lab users come from every possible background and from all over the world. Fab Lab projects can be an eye-opening hobby or they can produce life-changing innovations. For students, Fab Lab allows them literally to take learning into their own hands.

Fab Labs aim to make cutting-edge technology available to everyone. After initially concentrating on innovation and incubation of tech-oriented businesses, Fab Lab came to emphasize inclusiveness and broad access to the community as the franchise expanded. Today, education is a key focus of Fab Lab programs, as evidenced by the number of facilities based in high schools, colleges, institutes, and other educational institutions.

Fab Lab for All

In the early 2000s, concern began to grow among American business and government leaders over the condition of STEM

An Akron makerspace called synHAK provides space and tools for members to work on projects of all kinds, from crafts to robotics.

competence among young people. Tests showed that students lacked proficiency in these areas, and high school students tended to express a lack of interest in pursuing STEM careers despite a projected increase in career opportunity in these fields. Initiatives were passed to promote engagement in STEM subjects, including moves to recruit teachers, increase opportunities for hands-on activities, and target groups traditionally underrepresented in STEM occupations, such as women, minorities, and first generation Americans.

WHERE DO YOU FIND A FAB LAB?

Finding the Fab Lab closest to you is as easy as checking a single site on the internet. All Fab Labs worldwide are listed at the site https://www.fablabs.io/labs. Each entry includes a brief

description and a link. You can choose to view the list of Fab Labs in the United States alone and look for your state or city. If you don't want to scroll down the entire list of over a hundred entries, you can check the map to view Fab Lab locations.

As you scan the descriptive statements about the world's Fab Labs, you'll appreciate even more fully the program's broad reach. Fab Labs can be found in schools, museums, cultural institutions, and communities. Fab Labs typically provide resources geared toward students or the general public, but there are labs that specialize in biology research, maritime projects, ecodesign, textiles, architecture, and woodworking. Many cite a focus on design. A rural Kenyan lab aims to use local materials in projects benefiting the community. Slovakia's first Fab Lab describes itself as "space for materialize our dreams." An Italian lab has a "Cafè-lab" with food printing machines alongside its Fab Lab. A Florida lab is open to all, including "students, teachers, hobbyists, entrepreneurs, business owners, retirees, inventors." Some facilities describe themselves as mobile Fab Labs. Blurbs frequently mention innovation, collaboration, sharing of knowledge, creativity, STEM education, experimentation, prototyping, and entrepreneurship.

If there's no Fab Lab near your home, check the internet for makerspaces or hackerspaces in your area that are unaffiliated with Fab Lab. Local colleges or community centers may also have fabrication workshops that are open to the public.

Makerspaces have been established across the globe. Makespace Cambridge, in the United Kingdom, provides a space for British makers to get together and work on projects.

Fab Lab is well-qualified to advance enthusiasm and participation in STEM areas. All Fab Labs aim to expand knowledge, but some make education their core mission. They may develop their own curriculum or participate in a network such as FabLab@School, a concept developed by faculty at Stanford University. This program puts fabrication tools into students' hands, but just as important, it emphasizes problem solving, innovation, and collaboration rather than rote instruction from a teacher. Students learn through projects that spur them on to experiment, explore, and create. There is no single correct answer at the end of the project because each kid charts his or her own course, although the teacher helps guide students' progress.

Fab Lab projects are intended to appeal to students of all backgrounds, ages, and interests, not just those already disposed to studying engineering or science. Fab Lab is a creative enterprise. Some educators emphasize STEAM learning—science, technology, engineering, arts, and math—rather than just STEM topics. Schools traditionally separate arts programs from STEM instruction. The qualities typically associated with these different areas of learning, however, combine to bring about impressive results in a Fab Lab. Students working on tech and science projects benefit from creative and intuitive approaches. Students creating arts and crafts excel when they use problem solving and innovation in their projects.

As was mentioned, Fab Lab is a collaborative enterprise. But what does this mean in practice? People working in Fab Labs and other makerspaces aren't working completely alone even when they're concentrating on individual projects. In class, students help each other and offer encouragement, input, and feedback. Students don't automatically call for a teacher or

Fab Labs are collaborative spaces that welcome users of all ages, who bring enthusiasm for a variety of different types of interests.

supervisor when they're stuck—they may ask a peer for ideas first. In community spaces, Fab Labs bring together people from diverse backgrounds. Some enthusiasts decide to volunteer at their Fab Lab in order to share their knowledge with others. Online, makers share projects and designs, and they praise and ask for more information on other people's achievements.

THE FAB CHARTER

A charter is a formal agreement that grants certain rights to an institution. Charters are often complex, highly legalistic documents. The Fab Charter lists the conditions that a fabrication workshop must fulfill in order to qualify as a Fab Lab. Unlike typical charters, it's brief—less than a page in length—and focuses on practical considerations.

The document begins by defining a Fab Lab, its capabilities, and the resources it provides. It emphasizes how Fab Labs aim to provide access to the community and lists the responsibilities that a person or group setting up a Fab Lab has:

safety: not hurting people or machines
operations: assisting with cleaning, maintaining, and improving the lab
knowledge: contributing to documentation and instruction

Different Fab Labs tend to emphasize different missions. Some are primarily learning environments; others focus on entrepreneurs interested in business incubation. The charter supports the development of innovative new solutions while remaining committed to sharing knowledge and maintaining open access to Fab Labs. It includes the following questions and answers:

Who owns fab lab inventions?
Designs and processes developed in fab labs can be

protected and sold however an inventor chooses, but should remain available for individuals to use and learn from

How can businesses use a fab lab?

Commercial activities can be prototyped and incubated in a fab lab, but they must not conflict with other uses, they should grow beyond rather than within the lab, and they are expected to benefit the inventors, labs, and networks that contribute to their success

Getting Serious About Fab Lab

Fab Lab has grown in scope and sheer size since its early origins in the MIT classroom. There is now a Fab Lab Network that holds an annual symposium. The Fab Foundation supports a Fab City project that aims to develop a new urban model. MIT's Center for Bits and Atoms continues to perform groundbreaking research on topics from machines that make machines (http://mtm.cba.mit.edu) to programmable matter (http://milli.cba.mit.edu). Individual Fab Labs also promote research in a variety of different areas.

If you're a Fab Lab fanatic, you might consider applying to Fab Academy, an intensive five-month program that offers a diploma upon successful completion. Participants across the globe view lectures and complete the coursework in their local Fab Labs, and the course requires about a thirty hour time commitment each week. Tuition is not cheap, although some Fab Labs offer scholarships. Prospective students should already have a solid background in 2D and 3D modeling, digital fabrication, electronics programming, and web design and development. Lecture topics for 2016 include:

- Principles and practices
- Project management
- Computer-aided design
- Computer-controlled cutting
- Electronics production
- Computer-controlled machining
- Electronics design
- Molding and casting
- Composites
- Embedded programming
- 3D scanning and printing
- Input devices
- Interface and application programming
- Mechanical design
- Output devices
- Networking and communications
- Machine design
- Applications and implications
- Project development
- Invention, intellectual property, and income

Each week has an assignment, such as "design a 3D mold, machine it, and cast parts from it" or "make something big." Students must complete and present a final project.

You don't have to attend Fab Academy, pursue an engineering career, or start up your own tech company in order to benefit from a Fab Lab, however. Fab Labs are meant for everyone from students to hobbyists to hackers. It imparts knowledge that is transferable across different disciplines. Even if you're just a Fab Lab dabbler, you'll gain a degree of digital expertise without even realizing it. Fab Lab projects promote critical thinking and problem solving, as well as creativity, innovation, self-directed learning, and collaboration. Fab Lab experience will serve you well in many settings.

A Global Phenomenon

Fab Labs can be found around the world, and they have already made a difference globally. Fab Labs offer opportunities in poorer countries as well in as wealthy, developed nations. Every Fab Lab has the potential to provide educational opportunities and make a difference in a local community, but in some cases, work done in Fab Labs can be transformative. Children in a Ghana Fab Lab are manufacturing circuit boards. Fab Lab users in India are milling their own gears to repair outdated machines.

In 2010, various Fab Labs contributed to the creation of the Fab Lab House, designed by a Spanish architectural institute. The structure produces twice as much electricity as it uses. It is constructed out of pieces made by digital fabrication machines.

One of the more ambitious Fab Lab endeavors has been FabFi, a project undertaken in 2011 in Afghanistan. Basic infrastructure in the country, from power plants to schools, incurred damage during the most recent war. FabFi brought high-speed Internet to the city of Jalalabad using a network made up of nodes made up of cheap materials that, in some cases, can be scavenged from the trash.

Some experts have described the maker movement, combined with the advent of new high-tech fabrication methods,

The solar powered FabLab House—which contains its own small Fab Lab inside—is seen at night on June 22, 2010, in Madrid, Spain.

as the next industrial revolution. The internet has transformed marketplaces around the world, and desktop manufacturing has put advanced design and production capabilities in the hands of small-time inventors and entrepreneurs. Observers sometimes speculate about whether the day will come when consumers customize and make goods using their own personal fabrication machines rather than buying them premade. Commentators don't mention as often the sense of connection and community that is central to the maker movement, however. Fab Labs tend to draw attention for its cutting-edge ideas and machines, but at the heart of the movement are the people promoting innovation, learning, and collaborating for a brighter future.

Glossary

CAD Acronym for computer-aided design, the use of software and hardware in designing 2D and 3D drawings and models.

CAM Acronym for computer-aided manufacturing, the use of software to instruct a machine in the execution of a CAD design.

CNC milling machine A machine that mills items by carving away material from a larger piece using a computer controlled cutting tool.

CNC router A computer controlled machine that cuts and carves large sheets of wood and other material.

collaborate To work together or cooperate with others, especially in order to produce something.

computer science The branch of engineering that deals with computer hardware and software.

customize To modify in order to meet certain specifications or suit personal preferences.

entrepreneur An individual who organizes and operates a business, especially one that involves a financial risk.

Fab Lab A trademarked term referring to a workspace containing cutting-edge fabrication machines and electronics that supports educational and entrepreneurial applications in a collaborative setting.

fabricate To manufacture, construct, or build something.

G-Code A numerical control (NC) programming language used to control computerized machine tools.

innovate To invent or introduce something new.

laser cutter A machine that cuts and engraves plastic and other materials using a laser.

makerspace A workspace, often containing fabricating machines and other shop or craft equipment, where makers gather to create things and share knowledge and resources.

program Coded operations performed by a computer; also, to write these operations.

prototype An early model, such as of a manufactured item.

software The programs used to operate computers and related devices.

STEM Acronym for science, technology, engineering, and math.

3D printer A machine that prints 3D objects by applying numerous successive layers, usually of plastic, to build up the shape as designed.

vinyl cutter A machine that cuts shapes out of sheets of vinyl and other thin materials.

District 3 Innovation Center
6th Floor, 1250 Rue Guy
Montréal, QC H3H 2L3
Canada
info@d3center.ca
Website: http://d3center.ca

District 3 is an innovation and entrepreneurship zone at the heart of Concordia University. It includes a makerspace for development of prototypes that offers access to the community.

échoFab
355 Rue Peel, Suite 111
Montréal QC H3C 2G9
Canada
(514) 948-6644
Website: http://www.echofab.org

Established in 2011, ÉchoFab was Canada's first Fab Lab. Its website describes it as an "experimental digital fabrication laboratory."

Fab Central
Center for Bits and Atoms
20 Ames Street, E15-404
Cambridge, MA 02139
(617) 253-4651
Website: http://fab.cba.mit.edu

Fab Central supports a digital fabrication facility and global network of field Fab Labs managed by MIT's Center for Bits and Atoms.

Fab Foundation

50 Milk Street, 16th Floor

Boston, MA 02109

(857) 333-7777

Website: http://www.fabfoundation.org

The Fab Foundation was formed in 2009 to facilitate and
support both the growth of the international Fab Lab
network and the development of regional capacity-building
organizations.

Harvard University Graduate School of Design Fabrication Lab

48 Quincy Street

Gund Hall

Cambridge, MA 02138

(617) 495-1000

Website: http://www.gsd.harvard.edu/#/gsd-resources/
fabrication-laboratory

Harvard's Fab Lab features a wide range of equipment, from
cutting edge robotic arms, CNC routers and milling
machines, 3D printers, and laser cutters, to a traditional
wood-and-metal-working shop.

Make:

Maker Media

1160 Battery Street #125

San Francisco, CA 94111

(877) 306-6253

Website: http://makezine.com

Maker Media serves a growing community of makers who
bring a DIY mindset to technology to develop projects
that demonstrate how they can interact with the world
around them.

United States Fab Lab Network (USFLN)
2320 Renaissance Boulevard
Sturtevant, WI 53177
(262) 898-7430
Website: http://usfln.org
The USFLN is a connected network of Fab Labs that exchange knowledge, ideas, and resources to collectively empower people of all ages and backgrounds to experiment and invent new products to solve real world problems at local, national, and global levels.

Websites

Because of the changing nature of internet links, Rosen Publishing has developed an online list of websites related to the subject of this book. This site is updated regularly. Please use this link to access this list:

http://www.rosenlinks.com/GCFL/mill

Baichtal, John. *Hack This! 24 Incredible Hackerspace Projects from the DIY Movement.* Indianapolis, IN: Que, 2012.

Blikstein, Paulo (ed.), Sylvia Libow Martinez (ed.), and Heather Allen Pang (ed.). *Meaningful Making: Projects and Inspirations for Fab Labs and Makerspaces.* Torrance, CA: Constructing Modern Knowledge Press, 2016.

Cantor, Doug. *The Big Book of Hacks: 264 Amazing DIY Tech Projects.* San Francisco, CA: Weldon Owen, 2016.

Crawford, Matthew B. *Shop Class as Soulcraft: An Inquiry Into the Value of Work.* New York, NY: Penguin Press, 2009.

Doorley, Scott. *Make Space: How to Set the Stage for Creative Collaboration.* Hoboken, NJ: John Wiley & Sons, 2012.

Foege, Alec. *The Tinkerers The Amateurs, DIYers, and Inventors Who Make America Great.* New York, NY: Basic Books, 2013.

Hackett, Chris. *The Big Book of Maker Skills: Tools and Techniques for Building Great Tech Projects.* San Francisco, CA: Weldon Owen, 2014.

Harvey, James A. *CNC Trade Secrets: A Guide to CNC Machine Shop Practices.* 3rd ed. South Norwalk, CN: Industrial Press, 2014.

Hippel, Eric von. *Democratizing Innovation.* Cambridge, MA: MIT Press, 2005.

Instructables.com. *How to Do Absolutely Everything: Homegrown Projects from Do-It-Yourself Experts.* New York, NY: Skyhorse Publishing, 2014.

Kelly, Kevin. *Cool Tools: A Catalog of Possibilities.* Berkeley, CA: Publishers Group West, 2013.

For Further Reading

Kemp, Adam. *The Makerspace Workbench: Tools, Technologies, and Techniques for Making.* Sebastopol, CA: Maker Media, 2013.

Korn, Peter. *Why We Make Things and Why It Matters: The Education of A Craftsman*. Boston, MA: David R. Godine, 2013.

Lang, David. *Zero to Maker: Learn (Just Enough) to Make (Just About) Anything.* Sebastopol, CA: Maker Media, 2013.

Maietta, Andrea, and Paolo Aliverti. *The Maker's Manual: A Practical Guide to the New Industrial Revolution.* Sebastopol, CA: Maker Media, 2015.

Mongeon, Bridgette. *3D Technology in Fine Art and Craft: Exploring 3D Printing, Scanning, Sculpting and Milling.* Burlington, MA: Focal Press, 2015.

Smid, Peter. *CNC Tips and Techniques: A Reader for Programmers.* New York, NY: Industrial Press, 2013.

Werker, Kim Piper. *Make It Mighty Ugly: Exercises and Advice for Getting Creative Even When It Ain't Pretty.* Seattle, WA: Sasquatch Books, 2014.

Wilkinson, Karen, and Mike Petrich. *The Art of Tinkering: Meet 150+ Makers Working at the Intersection of Art, Science, and Technology.* San Francisco, CA: Weldon Owen, 2013.

Anderson, Chris. *Makers: The New Industrial Revolution*. New York, NY: Crown Business, 2012.

CNCCookbook. "Be a Better CNC'er." Retrieved May 9, 2016 (http://www.cnccookbook.com).

Educause. "7 Things You Should Know About Makerspaces." April 2013 (https://net.educause.edu/ir/library/pdf/eli7095.pdf).

Fab Academy. "FAQ." 2016 (http://fabacademy.org/faq).

Fab Central. "Fab Contract." Retrieved August 18, 2016 (http://fab.cba.mit.edu/about/charter/).

Fab Central. "Fab Lab FAQ." Retrieved May 9, 2016 (http://fab.cba.mit.edu/about/faq).

Fab Foundation. "Labs." 2015 (http://www.fabfoundation.org/fab-labs).

Fab Labs. "Fab Labs: Labs." 2016 (https://www.fablabs.io/labs).

Gershenfeld, Neil. "How to Make Almost Anything: The Digital Fabrication Revolution." *Foreign Affairs*, November/December 2012.

Hatch, Mark. *The Maker Movement Manifesto: Rules for Innovation in the New World of Crafters, Hackers, and Tinkerers*. New York, NY: McGraw Hill Education, 2014.

Koss, Nick. "3D CNC Milling: Choosing the Right Mill for Jewelry Work." CAD Jewellery Skills, September 3, 2013 (http://www.cadjewelleryskills.com/3d-cnc-milling-choosing -the-right-mill-for-jewelry-work).

Littlemachineshop.com. "CNCSoftware." Retrieved May 9, 2016 (https://www.littlemachineshop.com/Info/CNCSoftware.pdf).

Maker Faire. "Maker Faire." 2016 (http://makerfaire.com).

Miller, Andrew. "What Is a Makerspace?" Makerspaces.com. November 27, 2015 (https://www.makerspaces.com/ what-is-a-makerspace).

Museum of Science and Industry Chicago. "Dream It, Design It, Fab It!" 2016 (http://www.msichicago.org/explore/whats -here/tours-and-experiences/dream-it-design-it-fab-it).

Newcombe, Pat, and Nicole Belbin. "Fab Labs at the Library: Community 'Makerspaces' Give Access to Cutting-Edge Tools." Government Technology, September 25, 2012 (http://www.govtech.com/e-government/Fab-Labs--at-the -Library.html).

Nussbaum, Bruce. *Creative Intelligence: Harnessing the Power to Create, Connect, and Inspire.* New York, NY: Harper Business, 2013.

Proto Labs. "3D Printed, CNC Machined, or Molded Prototypes: Which and When?" February 2013 (https://www.protolabs

.com/resources/injection-molding-design-tips/united
-states/2013-02).

Rodriguez, Luis. "Get Acquainted with CNC Machining." *Make:*,
December 9, 2015 (http://makezine.com/2015/12/09/get
-acquainted-cnc-machining).

Roland DGA Corporation. "Rapid Prototyping Machines." 2016
(https://www.rolanddga.com/applications/rapid-prototyping).

Stanford Graduate School of Education. "FabLab@School:
Transformative Learning Technologies Lab." 2013 (https://
tltl.stanford.edu/project/fablabschool).

Ungerleider, Neal. "Afghanistan's Amazing DIY Internet." Fast
Company, June 21, 2011 (http://www.fastcompany.com/
1761891/afghanistans-amazing-diy-Internet).

Index

About the Author

Jason Porterfield is a writer and journalist living in Chicago. He writes about tech subjects for several publications. His technology titles for Rosen Publishing include *Julian Assange and Wikileaks, Niklas Zennström and Skype, Tech Pioneers: Tim Berners-Lee,* and *Conducting Basic and Advanced Searches*. In his spare time, he enjoys tinkering with old bicycles.

Photo Credits

Cover RomboStudio/Shutterstock.com; p. 5 Lilyana Vynogradova/Shutterstock.com; p. 7 Michael Haegele/Fuse/Getty Images; p. 9 Pacific Press/LightRocket/Getty Images; pp. 13, 21 © AP Images; p. 15 Museum of Science and Industry, Chicago/Archive Photos/Getty Images; p. 17 amixstudio/Shutterstock.com; p. 23 Fernando Blanco Calzada/Shutterstock.com; p. 24 Monkey Business Images/Shutterstock.com; p. 28 clu/E+/Getty Images; p. 31 SNEHIT/Shutterstock.com; p. 33 Garsya/Shutterstock.com; p. 35 mavo/Shutterstock.com; p. 38 Altzone/Wikimedia Commons/Open Source Hardware (OSHW) Logo on blank PCB.jpg/CC BY-SA 3.0; p. 41 Tribune Content Agency LLC/Alamy Stock Photo; pp. 42-43 Laura James/Flickr/ https://www.flickr.com/photos/lauriej/8827010024/CC BY 2.0; p. 45 © iStockphoto.com/Steve Debenport; pp. 50-51 Denis Doyle/Getty Images; cover and interior pages background pattern Slanapotam/Shutterstock.com.

Designer: Nicole Russo; Editor: Bernadette Davis;
Photo Researcher: Nicole DiMella